A Journey
Through Affliction

A Devotional Guide To Hope

PHYLLIS A. CLEMONS

INSPIRED PRESS PUBLISHER

Scripture quotations are from The Holy Bible, English Standard Version®

(ESV®), copyright ©2001 by Crossway, a publishing ministry of Good News Publishers. Used by permission. All rights reserved.

Scripture quotations taken from the New American Standard Bible ®

Copyright ©1960, 1962, 1963, 1968, 1971, 1972, 1973, 1975, 1977, 1995 by The Lockman Foundation. Used by permission. (**www.Lockman.org**)

Scriptures taken from the Holy Bible, New International Version ®, NIV®.

Copyright ©1973, 1978, 1984, 2011 by Biblica, Inc.™ Used by permission of Zondervan. All rights reserved worldwide. **www.zondervan.com** The "NIV" and "New International Version" are trademarks registered in the United States Patent and Trademark Office by Blibilica, Inc. ™ All rights reserved.

Scriptures taken from the King James Version of the Bible.

Inspried Press Publisher

1333 Chelsea Court

Morrow, OH 45152

www.inspiredpresspublisher.com

513-256-1792

ISBN: 978-0-692-67131-3

Library of Congress Control Number: 2016936603

Dedication

This book is dedicated to my husband,

Randall James Clemons.

I am blessed by your unconditional love.

Thank you for your patience, gentleness, and faithfulness.

Thank you for walking with me through every storm.

Thank you for being my companion on this journey.

Preface

Life is a journey and we are all travelers. The course of everyone's journey differs in content and length, but the destination is the same – transformation into the image of God's beloved Son, Jesus the Messiah. To reach that destination, God invites us to join Him in relationship where He imparts truth, wisdom, and revelation for a greater understanding of His characteristics.

The journey is full of the unknown. We experience exhilaration and upheaval, warfare and times of rest, but through it all God remains the same.

The first time God whispered the words *broken-wing* to me was for the purpose of writing about my journey from spiritual brokenness to spiritual maturity. This time, though I am still on the journey, those same words take on a slightly different meaning. This time *broken-wing* represents my journey through physical affliction.

This is an expose' of my journey. On the pages that follow, I have captured some of the most important truths and revelations that God blessed me with while traveling through one of the most difficult seasons of my life.

With Him, I've learned to stand even though I did not experience an instantaneous miracle. I have embraced the power of process. And in that process, I have been awestruck by His grace. I have learned the beauty of living my life at a pace that was once foreign. I have captured the very essence of the disciplines of prayer and worship. In my weakness, I have discovered the true meaning of mounting up on eagles' wings. And I understand the relevance of the glory of God being revealed through my life.

Perhaps your journey through affliction has just begun or maybe you have been traveling this road for a very long time. In either case, living with a *broken-wing* is not easy or pleasant, but it offers many opportunities. As you travel your unique journey, it is my prayer that you will allow God to meet you at every point. May you be comforted by His peace and filled with His joy. May your heart be touched by His unfailing love for you.

Acknowledgments

During this journey, I have had the unique privilege of being in the company of many caring people. They have offered comfort and encouragement. They have interceded in prayer. They have lent their shoulders as I have cried. They have restored my hope and brought me joy.

To my sister Jean, thank you for your quiet strength as you faced the debilitating effects of your own physical affliction. I will always cherish your love and support. I miss you. Rest in peace until Christ comes again.

To my cousin Brenda, thank you for standing tall as you too faced the challenges of physical affliction. You are truly an example of perseverance in the face of adversity.

To my mother, Hattie Carr, thank you for your encouragement, prayers, and support. Thank you for loving me unconditionally. Thank you for carrying me in your womb, and for birthing me into this world. Through you, I arrived to serve the Living God. Your journey through affliction was brief but intense. Yet, even in your suffering you remained a symbol of strength. You knew the Lord was coming for you and you were prepared for the transition from this earthly life. When I held your hand for the last time I was at peace knowing that you were going to meet the King of Kings. You fought a good fight, and eternal life is your reward. Your 97-year legacy will always be cherished. Thank you, Mom, for everything.

To my family members and friends, thanks to all of you for your prayers and support.

To Mary Busha, thank you for seeing the book project in a new light and encouraging me to expand the ministry of writing. Thank you for working so diligently to help bring this devotional to completion.

To Felisha A. Cook, thank you for your gift of artistic design in the creation of the cover.

Contents

Introduction

"Your eyes saw my unformed body; all the days ordained for me were written in your book before one of them came to be." Psalm 139:16, NIV

Mankind's days are often referred to as a life-span. It is the number of years of our earthly existence. Through our life-span, we all have experiences. Experiences are fragments of the whole. Experiences are the various personal encounters that grow us, stretch us, prune us, and rearrange us. They can become opportunities for gaining knowledge, wisdom, and skills.

Experiences are the content of stories that are told or written. Some experiences become biographies, autobiographies, documentaries, movies, news headlines, magazine articles, or are contained within portions of various types of published books. Volumes of materials have been recorded based on the human experience.

The gospels evolved from stories of the human experience passed down through oral tradition before acquiring their literary form. It was the human experience communicated through oral tradition that Luke investigated before he wrote what he calls an orderly account to Theophilus, known as the gospel of Luke (see Luke 1:1-4).

Experiences can be memorable times of laughter, joy, and excitement, but also they can be miserable, perplexing, and challenging. Having a *broken-wing* can be classified as a miserable, perplexing, and challenging experience. If we perceive that it is an evil disruption and for our demise, we may respond in despair. This may cause us to isolate ourselves from the world and simply give up on pursuing the abundant life in Christ. Erroneously, we may believe that God has forsaken us. If on the other hand, we perceive that the miserable, perplexing and challenging experiences may be tools for our spiritual growth and for His glory, then we may respond with a renewed and even greater hope in God who is faithful in the midst of it all.

This devotional has been written as a compass to guide you through the affliction you are experiencing. I pray that you will find encouragement, strength, and hope as you read its contents, respond to the questions, and write out your personal prayers.

I

An Unexpected Cross

"I have been crucified with Christ. It is no longer I who live, but Christ who lives in me. And the life I now live in the flesh I live by faith in the Son of God, who loved me and gave himself for me." Galatians 2:20

I was partially awake that night, but I was stirred to attention when I heard the voice of a woman on a Christian television broadcast say, "Unexpected crosses."

"So that's what this is called," I thought. I had known some type of stormy season was approaching and that I was well into the journey, but I hadn't expected one of this nature.

It was about mid-2004 when I began to sense that I would soon face a trial of some type. I tried to dismiss my feelings, but the kindling in my heart let me know that this season of my life was imminent. It was confirmed when I heard the Father gently whisper. "There is one more thing I have to take you through."

I spent a fair amount of time thinking about it and even became fearful of the unknown. I had no details, no strategies, no timeline, and no idea of the outcome. But something was on the horizon. It would be one of the longest journeys I had ever taken. I would later name it "an unexpected cross."

I was getting the impression that this unexpected cross would somehow be related to physical affliction, but I didn't know who was involved. When two of my close family members were diagnosed with serious illnesses, I thought perhaps this was the imminent season to which God was referring. I later discovered it was only a portion of it.

Later that year, I began to experience problems with my jaw. I noticed that every car commute caused my jaw to shift slightly to the left, and after arriving at my destination I was fatigued. When I retired for the night, I had great difficulty getting comfortable because I could not get my jaw to relax and rest in its normal position. By the time I finally drifted off to sleep, I was exhausted, but thankful for the temporary escape from the rising discomfort.

Thinking something may have happened following the completion of some recent dental work, I made an appointment to see my dentist. He referred me to an orthodontist. After all of the preliminary examinations, he recommended and placed me in braces as a partial solution to the problem. He also informed me that jaw surgery would be necessary. I dismissed the recommendation and ignored his intermittent promptings to contact the surgeon. Instead, I prayed and made positive declarations from God's word, such as "I am the Lord that healeth thee" (Exodus 15:26, KJV). I fought with all my might for God to heal me.

Despite my prayers and declarations of faith, the physical battle heightened. The pain became constant due to the headaches and muscle spasms that ran from my jaw and up the left side of my head. Temporary relief from the spasms was only possible by holding my jaw in its proper position. To perform activities that required the use of both hands, such as cooking, I braced my lower jaw with my left shoulder to minimize the spasms and movement.

Reflections of the Journey:

1. If you are currently carrying an unexpected cross in the form of a physical affliction, describe what it is and how you feel about it.

_____

_____

_____

_____

_____

_____

_____

2. At this time, what steps are you taking to deal with your affliction?

_____

_____

_____

_____

_____

_____

_____

_____

Prayer for the Journey:

_____

_____

_____

_____

_____

_____

_____

_____

_____

_____

_____

_____

2

Like a Ship in the Storm

"This is my comfort in my affliction, that your promise gives me life." Psalm 119:50

Over a period of time, the shape of my face became somewhat distorted. My lower jaw began to protrude and my face twisted to the left. My ability to speak was affected and it became necessary to limit and sometimes withdraw from activities that required a lot of conversation. Eating meals was difficult due to the improper alignment of my upper and lower jaws. Performing everyday activities was like trying to be still while operating a jack hammer.

At the time, I was serving in a position in the marketplace that I thoroughly enjoyed. However, my ability to perform my tasks at optimum capacity was also hindered by the amplifying affliction.

In the presence of others, such as coworkers, family, and friends, I tried to hide the agony of this affliction. I wanted to stand tall and not allow this cross to consume my life. I felt that I needed to push past it and pray, and that it would soon go away. Despite my prayers and the prayers of others on my behalf, the healing I desperately desired escaped me. The journey would be longer than I had anticipated.

After several months, I was physically and mentally exhausted. Finally, I conceded to the orthodontist's recommendation to contact the surgeon. The surgical procedure would require breaking and repositioning my jaw. It would be several more months before the surgery was actually performed, however.

I counted down the months, weeks, and days. "The end is in sight," I kept saying to myself. I was hopeful the surgery would put an end to this fiery trial and that my life would return to normal.

While waiting, I kept my prayer vigil for a miraculous healing. The time passed, however, and there was no miracle. As a result, many thoughts and questions entered my mind. I wondered if my faith was too small. Did I need to wait a little longer? Should I forgo the surgery? God is all-powerful and quite capable of healing me without surgery, but He chose not to. I couldn't then and may never be able to explain why.

So on that beautiful, sunny July day, I arrived at the hospital to undergo what was supposed to put an end to the affliction. At first, the surgery seemed to be a success, but about a week or so afterwards, once again, my jaw began to shift to the left. This was accompanied by pain on the left side of my head and the spasms were worse than before.

The medical recommendation was to take me back to surgery, remove the steel pins that held my jaw in place, reposition my jaw, and wire my mouth shut so that my jaw would not move. Fifteen days later, I was back in surgery.

I trusted that this surgery would prove to be successful. However, it was followed by more excruciating pain. It resembled sailing on a small ship in a violent storm. Just as the waves of water pound against a ship's hull, tossing it wildly in the waters, the pain (that intensified with any movement) came in waves so severe that it knocked me to my knees. This certainly was not the cross I was expecting.

Reflections of the Journey:

1. Have you experienced hope in your healing only to have disappointment follow close behind? If so, how did you handle it?

_____

_____

_____

_____

_____

_____

_____

_____

2. It has been proven that writing about your feelings and experiences brings a level of healing. Consider taking a few moments now (or very soon) to write about your affliction and how it makes you feel. This writing is for your eyes only, so be honest and don't worry about grammar or punctuation.

_____

_____

_____

_____

_____

_____

Prayer for the Journey:

_____

_____

_____

_____

_____

_____

_____

_____

_____

_____

_____

_____

3

Exhausted but Moving Forward

"But we have this treasure in jars of clay, to show that the surpassing power belongs to God and not to us. We are afflicted in every way, but not crushed, perplexed, but not driven to despair, persecuted, but not forsaken; struck down, but not destroyed; always carrying in the body the death of Jesus, so that the life of Jesus may so be manifested in our bodies." 2 Corinthians 4:7-10

During the weeks and months that followed, I was treated with heavy medication. Subsequently, I was referred to another specialist for pain disorder in my head and neck. After being under his care for several months, some of the intense pain subsided.

I then learned that my jaw was locked. The surgeon performed several in-office treatments in an attempt to unlock it, but it wouldn't budge. Three months later, in November 2006, a third, much simpler surgery was performed. It proved successful, and my jaw opening expanded. I was grateful for that small step.

What I couldn't seem to find out was why the involuntary jaw movement and spasms had not ceased. In addition, I was constantly biting my tongue and the sides of my cheeks. I would almost scream each time, because it was uncontrollable and painful. The motion of riding in a car was nearly unbearable. The commutes left me feeling as if I had been violently shaken.

My speech was slurred and sometimes it was difficult for others to understand me. Needless to say, I was often frustrated and would get upset with my husband, Randall, or my mom when I had to repeat what I had just struggled to communicate.

I continued to limit the length and types of activities I engaged in. Sleep and frequent rest periods proved to be good medicine. It was not until April of 2007 that I began to regain some strength, but the fight to regain total health continued.

I continued to pray, seeking God for total healing. I remember the specialist who treated me mentioning that the problems I was experiencing were due to a disorder in my central nervous system. Finally, following the leading of the Holy Spirit, I sought out the help of a neurologist who ordered a brain scan and blood work.

The diagnosis was Oromandibular Dystonia. How it came about, no one knows. The prognosis: There is no cure. This would medically explain all of the physical symptoms and fatigue, which I learned was caused by my body having to keep up with the constant muscle movement and contractions. Having received this diagnosis, I began a new series of treatments. After several months, I began to experience some relief. Although I am not totally healed, I am joyfully grateful for the wonderful progress.

Living with a *broken-wing* is physically, mentally, emotionally, and spiritually exhausting. Despite the mystery of what has taken place, the challenges I have lived through and that may lie ahead, I am determined to move forward. I will not forsake my God. My faith has been and will continue to be tested over and over again. The experiences of this season have been and continue to be a tool for my spiritual growth, and in due season I will reap a spiritual harvest that will bring glory to God. The season for reaping will require that I remain steadfast and patient because this experience of "an unexpected cross" is about process.

Reflections of the Journey:

1. List ways in which your unexpected cross have limited you in any way:

_____

_____

_____

_____

_____

_____

_____

2. Can you see how God can use what you're going through as a spiritual tool in your life? Explain.

_____

_____

_____

_____

_____

_____

_____

_____

_____

_____

Prayer for the Journey:

_____

_____

_____

_____

_____

_____

_____

_____

_____

_____

_____

4

The Power of Process

" 'Remember the former things of old; for I am God, and there is no other; I am God, and there is none like me, declaring the end from the beginning and from ancient times things not yet done, saying, 'My counsel shall stand, and I will accomplish all my purpose.' "
Isaiah 46:9-10

What did the woman who had the issue of blood for twelve years, the invalid of thirty-eight years at the pool of Bethesda, and the woman who because of an infirmity had been bent over for eighteen years have in common? They all had a *broken-wing* – an affliction that had been a part of their lives for an extensive period of time – and after a brief encounter with the Messiah, they were healed. Jesus' authority over sickness and disease was evident. In addition, prior to receiving their miraculous healing, each of them endured a process.

Ancients in Process

It is the sketches of the lives of these ancient heroes in process that inspire me as I have journeyed through my own affliction. I am moved by their perseverance and faith. I am even intrigued by the unwritten details of their experiences.

The gospel narratives do not chronicle the complete details of the lives of the woman with the issue of blood, the invalid at the pool of Bethesda, or the woman who had been bent over for eighteen years prior to their miraculous healings. I do wonder, however, what they dealt with mentally and emotionally as they rose to face the challenges that accompanied their infirmities. How did they deal with the reality of physical differences, the limitation in activity, and in some cases exclusion from the mainstreams of society? How were they impacted economically? What was the state of their soul? Let's take a look at the life sketches of two of them.

She is often referred to as "The woman with the issue of blood." She was among the multitude as Jesus and the disciples departed from the boat after crossing the Sea of Galilee. She had suffered from her affliction for twelve long years. She had sought medical attention from various sources none of which brought her relief, her funds were depleted, and her condition worsened. According to the Torah she was considered unclean:

"If a woman has a discharge of blood for many days, not at the time of her menstrual impurity, or if she has a discharge beyond the time of her impurity, all the days of the discharge she shall continue in uncleanness. As in the days of her impurity, she shall be unclean. Every bed on which she lies, all the days of her discharge, shall be to her as the bed of her impurity. And everything on which she sits shall be unclean, as in the uncleanness of her menstrual impurity. And whoever touches these things shall be unclean, and shall wash his clothes and bathe himself in water and be unclean until the evening. But if she is cleaned of her discharge, she shall count for herself seven days, and after that she shall be clean. And on the eighth day she shall take two turtledoves or two pigeons and bring them to the priest, to the entrance of the tent of meeting. And the priest shall use one for a sin offering and the other for a burnt offering. And the priest shall make atonement for her before the LORD for her unclean discharge. " (Leviticus 15:25-30)

Because of the Levitical law and the clear distinction between "unclean" and "clean," both her personal and her communal life were affected. The law set the parameters. If the Israelites failed to observe these regulations, it could result in their dying in their unclean condition and the defilement of the tabernacle (see Leviticus 15:31). Contact with her surrounding community was risky to a nation that was being taught to separate themselves in order to establish a life of holiness.

"Speak to all the congregation of the people of Israel and say to them, You shall be holy, for I the LORD your God am holy." (Leviticus 19:2)

In addition to the physical discomfort of hemorrhaging, I would imagine that she experienced a fair amount of mental and emotional anguish. She may have wrestled with shame, rejection, loneliness, depression, hopelessness, and distress.

Undeterred by the limitations placed upon her by the Levitical law and the pressure of her personal pain, on the pivotal day that Jesus reached the western shores of the Sea of Galilee, a desperate woman, propelled by her faith, made her way to Jesus. She had reached the point of human extremity. Moved by the good news about the Messiah's power to heal, she reached into the crowd and touched His garment, "And He said to her, 'Daughter, your faith has made you well; go in peace, and be healed of your disease' " (Mark 5:34).

Suddenly her life was transformed. The bleeding woman, once considered unclean, undesirable, and untouchable by others was accepted by Christ. He called her "Daughter." Through the demonstration of her faith in Him, she was adopted into the family of God. The "fountain of blood" suddenly stopped flowing. Jesus declared that she was "whole," meaning that her health was completely restored. She would need no other physician.

Finally, Jesus told her, "Go in peace." I believe He was addressing the state of her soul. Having suffered in her body for many years,

He was assuring her that she need not concern herself with this infirmity ever again. Her soul could finally be at rest.

Reflections of the Journey:

1. Like the woman in the crowd who may have felt shame, rejection, loneliness, depression, hopelessness, and distress, describe any of these feelings you may be experiencing.

_____

_____

_____

_____

_____

_____

_____

_____

2. Can you, like the woman in the crowd, reach out in boldness to the Lord for His healing touch and rest for your weary soul?

_____

_____

_____

_____

_____

_____

_____

Prayer for the Journey:

_____

_____

_____

_____

_____

_____

_____

_____

_____

_____

_____

5

The Man at the Pool

"Get up, take up your bed, and walk." John 5:8

Near the sheep gate, there was a pool in the city of Jerusalem named Bethesda. The spring-fed pool contained five porches and "in these lay a multitude of those who were sick, blind, lame, and withered [waiting for the moving of the waters]" (John 5:3, NASB). Though ancient manuscripts make no references to the pool being stirred by angels, it was a traditional belief that the waters had curative powers. Among those waiting for its moving was an infirmed man, weak and sick; he was an invalid.

It is highly probable that he also suffered mental and emotional anguish. He may have been oppressed by thoughts and feelings such as defeatism, exclusion, and unworthiness.

It was time for the feast of the Jews; Jesus and the disciples had come to the city of Jerusalem to celebrate. When Jesus saw the man who had been suffering with his infirmity for 38 years, He asked: "Do you want to be healed?" (John 5:6).

Having been ill for such an extended period of time, it almost seemed like a frivolous question. Frivolous, however, it was not. Rather, I would consider the Messiah's question was not only an expression of His unfailing compassion, but also it was provocative in nature. It was a question that challenged the invalid's faith and traditional beliefs about the curative powers of the pool's water. After hearing the man's verbal response, "Sir, I have no one to put me into the pool when the water is stirred up, and while I am going another steps down before me." Then Jesus gives the man a divine directive: "Get up, take up your bed, and walk" (John 5:7-8). His immediate healing came as he responded in faith.

The Messiah, defying legalism about breaking the Sabbath, blessed him with freedom and exhorted him to walk in sinlessness. Like the woman in the crowd, this man pushed past the pain and pressed into the extraordinary power and authority of the Master Physician.

Reflections of the Journey:

1. Are you, like the man at the pool, waiting for someone other than Jesus, or a circumstance, to be instrumental in your healing?

_____

_____

_____

_____

2. Whether or not the Lord brings you a miraculous healing like He did the man at the pool, are you willing to push through the pain of your affliction into the extraordinary power and authority of the Master Physician?

_____

_____

_____

_____

_____

Prayer for the Journey:

_____

_____

_____

_____

_____

_____

_____

_____

_____

_____

_____

6

Looking Beyond the Physical

"If a man dies, will he live again?" Job 14:14

The woman in the crowd and the man at the pool endured an extensive and tedious process before they were made well. I would imagine that both of them had thoughts and feelings that vacillated between hopelessness and hope. In hopelessness, they may have settled for the belief that deliverance was highly improbable. Their internal dialogue may have sounded a bit like this: "It does not appear that I am going to get better. I suppose I will have to deal with this infirmity for all of my remaining days." In hope, they may have adopted a conviction similar to Job's: "If a man dies, will he live again? All the days of my struggle I will wait until my change comes: (Job 14:14; NASB). With that conviction, they would have clung to a hope, believing that healing and restoration were just a matter of time.

We know the end of the story for both of them. For many of us, however, a question remains unanswered – how is this going to turn out? We have waited. The journey through affliction has been longer than anticipated. Life as we once knew it is becoming more of a distant memory.

Suffering with a *broken-wing* goes beyond the physical atrocities. It often includes the silent and invisible storms of mental and emotional anguish. Throughout the journey, we may sway between hopelessness and hope. The pain can be deep, intrusive, and immobilizing.

On May 20, 2007, I went through one of my many despairing moments. On that day I made the following journal entry:

When God? When will I ever get relief from this infirmity? What is the lesson?

How can I continue to function when I am constantly dealing with a weakness, an infirmity that just doesn't seem to want to go away? I know I must fight, but am I fighting correctly? What do I say? What do I do? I am not sure, so I am here for you to speak to me. I feel like my life is in shambles.

I need a breakthrough of the greatest kind. Why would you call me to teach your word and then allow the enemy to attack the part of my body that is utilized to assist me in carrying the message? I just don't understand. I have repented, fasted, prayed and waited, but the full manifestation of my healing has not come forth. When, God, when?

When and why? Those were the big questions for me. At that moment, I had not embraced the relevance of process. I was not thinking about how this journey through affliction could bring glory to God or further my spiritual growth. I just wanted a right-now deliverance!

What is interesting is that three months prior, on February 10, 2007, my thoughts and feelings were on the opposite side of the spectrum. I experienced an exciting and powerful moment of hope. On that day, I made this entry:

While it is true that recovery is draining, and can sometimes leave me feeling defeated, I can't live in that place, for to remain is to forego the opportunity to live in the place of peace. Rather, I must rise to a place where the effects of the affliction that I am experiencing in the natural no longer control my emotions, hinder my determination, or interrupts my pursuit of the plans God has for me.

I was empowered by God's spirit. I felt hope rising on the inside of me. My heart was set and my mind was focused on the one and only God – the same Messiah who healed the woman in the crowd and the man at the pool of Bethesda. My wing was still broken and the question of how all of this was going to turn out remained. But I had embraced the process. I recognized that a much greater work was being done inside my heart.

Reflections of the Journey:

1. What type of *broken-wing* are you dealing with?

_____

_____

_____

_____

_____

_____

_____

_____

_____

_____

_____

_____

2. How has the nature of your affliction affected your emotions, thoughts, and feelings?

_____

_____

_____

_____

_____

_____

3. What do you want Jesus do to for you?

_____

_____

_____

_____

_____

_____

4. Are you willing to embrace the process?

_____

_____

_____

_____

_____

_____

Prayer for the Journey:

_____

_____

_____

_____

_____

_____

_____

_____

_____

_____

_____

7

Embracing the Process

"The steadfast love of the Lord never ceases; his mercies never come to an end." Lamentations 3:22

I assume that you have responded to the questions at the end of the last devotion and that you are willing to embrace the process. So, how do we achieve victory in the midst of the fierce battles of affliction? How can we turn sorrow into joy and disappointments into opportunities? How do we remain poised when dealing with uncertainties? How do we keep ourselves from being overtaken by the various vacillating thoughts and feelings that go along with living with a *broken-wing*? How do we embrace the process?

The simple answer is that we must focus on God (gaining greater knowledge about His character) by seeking the wisdom and revelation that comes by His Spirit, and found in His Word, and not on our affliction. What makes it simple?

It's simple because God is full of mercy. "Blessed be the God and Father of our Lord Jesus Christ, the Father of mercies and God of all comfort" (2 Corinthians 1:3).

Jesus responded to a cry for mercy when blind Bartimaeus called out to Him as He and His disciples were leaving the city of Jericho: "And they came to Jericho. And as he was leaving Jericho with his disciples and a great crowd, Bartimaeus, a blind beggar, the son of Timaeus, was sitting by the roadside. And when he heard that it was

Jesus of Nazareth, he began to cry out and say, 'Jesus, Son of David, have mercy on me!' " (Mark 10:46-47).

Amidst the words of the lamenting prophet Jeremiah, we find a declaration of his trust in God:

"The steadfast love of the Lord never ceases; his mercies never come to an end; they are new every morning; great is your faithfulness. 'The Lord is my portion,' says my soul,' therefore I will hope in him' " (Lamentations 3:22-24).

It's simple because God is faithful. "Know therefore that the Lord your God is God, the faithful God who keeps covenant and steadfast love with those who love him and keep his commandments, to a thousand generations." (Deuteronomy 7:9).

"God is faithful, by whom you were called into the fellowship of his Son, Jesus Christ our Lord" (1 Corinthians 1:9).

"The Lord sustains him on his sickbed; in his illness you restore him to full health" (Psalm 41:3).

It's simple because the Word is true. The Word never fails. The Word gives life. David writes: "This is my comfort in my affliction, that your promise gives me life" (Psalm 119:50).

Despite the truths and promises found in the Word, maintaining our focus on God and not on our affliction is often met with opposition. The opposition, both internal and external, adds a great deal of complexity to the journey. So what makes the simple (focusing on God alone) complex?

It's complex because we sometimes allow our cares and anxiety over our circumstances prevent the Word from taking root in our hearts. If the Word is not rooted, its impact is only temporal.

It's complex because of the human struggle of looking beyond affliction. Mountains just in front of us are always easier to see than what is on the other side of them. We are instructed to speak to these massive obstructions and they will be moved (see Matthew 17:20). In many instances, however, despite the prayers offered to God and the declarations of faith spoken, mysteriously, they remain erect. Thus, we become discouraged.

It's complex because our minds can become consumed with questions of why and what led to this season of affliction. Why am I here, God? What did I do wrong" Why haven't you answered?

It's complex because our faith sometimes collides with fear, doubt, and unbelief.

It's *complex* because of the very practical challenges that arise out of physical affliction such as deferred dreams and vision, financial setbacks, and altered plans.

Whether we find striving to maintain our focus on God simple, complex, or somewhere in between, the key to achieving it is making a wholehearted commitment to our relationship with Him. It means remaining prayerful and bathing ourselves in the Word. It means pushing through the crowds to experience the wonderment of meeting God in silence and solitude. It means worshipping Him with a sincere heart. A wholehearted relationship requires one more thing – trust. Here is what I entered into my journal on November 11, 2007:

Perfect trust is trusting God when I can't see, when I don't know all of the answers, and when I don't know what is ahead of me nor the details of my tomorrows. Lord, I trust you. The better thing for me to say is that I am learning to trust and depend on you.

Reflections of the Journey:

1. Why do you think that embracing the process is simple? Why is it complex?

_____

_____

_____

_____

_____

_____

_____

_____

2. Have you made a wholehearted commitment to your relationship with the Lord? If not, are you willing to make that commitment now?

_____

_____

_____

_____

_____

_____

_____

_____

Prayer for the Journey:

_____

_____

_____

_____

_____

_____

_____

_____

_____

_____

8

Victory Through
the Process

"And I am sure of this, that he who began a good work in you will bring it to completion at the day of Jesus Christ." Philippians 1:6

Process always has a purpose. It is a common thread that runs through the lives of all of humanity. Process, in general, is directed toward some end and is applicable to many of life's arenas. I would describe process as a series of events, experiences, or circumstances throughout the course of one's life-span that are ultimately designed to bring about conversion and perpetual spiritual transformation. Process is used by God to set and keep us on the path to fulfill His foreordained purposes in and through our live. God uses process to bring us to completion.

Victory is normally equated with winning, conquest, or triumph over opposing forces. For the woman in the crowd, it was a dried up fountain of blood; for the man at the pool of Bethesda, it was walking; and for the bent-over woman, it was experiencing life in an upright position.

So how do we define victory when we are still going through the process? What is victory if we are still lame, still hemorrhaging, or still bent over? What is victory if our healing is not the picture-perfect image we had in mind? It is receiving in our hearts a revelation of who God is. He is faithful. He protects. He comforts. He strengthens. He is eternal, knowing the end from the beginning.

Victory through the process is embracing its power to work one of the greatest miracles of all times – the spiritual transformation that takes place in the heart.

Never doubt the Messiah's power to heal and restore you whether it is physical, emotional, mental, spiritual, or all of the above. Lift up your soul unto the Lord, gaze your eyes upon Him who is enthroned in heaven. You are not defeated…you are simply in process.

Reflections of the Journey:

1. Define what the word *victory* means to you.

_____

_____

_____

_____

_____

_____

_____

_____

_____

_____

_____

2. Can you embrace the statement that "You are not defeated…you are simply in process"?

_____

_____

_____

_____

_____

_____

_____

Prayer for the Journey:

_____

_____

_____

_____

_____

_____

_____

_____

_____

_____

9

Life in the Slow Lane

"And I will lead the blind in a way that they do not know, in paths that they have not known I will guide them. I will turn the darkness before them into light, the rough places into level ground. These are the things I do, and I do not forsake them." Isaiah 42:16

Process introduces a pace. Pace is the rate at which we move through the process. It is the tempo required for perpetual spiritual perfection. Because of God's love for us, He will often introduce circumstances which are designed to get us into the natural rhythms of kingdom life. If we allow Him, God will set the pace in our lives because ultimately He wants to guide us.

The March of the Geese

A few years ago in Southwestern Ohio, we began to see a migration of geese like never before. Wherever there was water, they would land and there they would either mingle along the earthen shores or elegantly glide across the glistening water. Being a lover of animals, I found them fascinating to watch. They have a graceful beauty I really admire.

I must admit, however, that my first personal encounter with these long-necked creatures was a bit annoying. I was traveling westbound by car on a weekday morning when the traffic came to a sudden halt. Crossing the street were several of these feathered spectacles and a lady in the middle of the street shooing them along. Oblivious to the disruption in the traffic flow, their only response was quacking and the flapping of wings. The lady's effort, though commendable, did not speed up the process; we still had to wait until they had all crossed the street before we could resume our commute.

Years later, during a lunchtime commute, I had to stop my car as a small delegation of geese leisurely strolled across the street to get to a nearby pond. This time, however, I gained a different perspective. Instead of getting agitated by having to wait for them to get to the other side, I began to think about the value they bring to the hurried human world. For me, it was a figurative reminder from God to "slow down."

Geese will not allow anyone to set the pace of life for them. A leisurely stroll in the middle of traffic seems normal for them. They are never in a hurry and are unaffected by roaring motors, turning wheels, blowing horns, or shouts from car windows. No expressions of road rage will encourage these winged creatures to pick up the pace. As I sat and waited, I chuckled, thinking, "God has a wonderful sense of humor."

This brought to my remembrance a message God had given me early on in my journey through affliction. Right after my first surgery and before the second, I attended a one-day retreat. Physically I was weak and in great discomfort, but I felt the need to push beyond it. I sensed that God had a message for me. Much to my surprise, the subject for the day was "Life in the Slow Lane."[1] As soon as I heard this phrase, I knew it was God speaking. I began to understand that this season of physical affliction was, in part, about slowing down.

---

1   The title of this chapter came from the topic at a "Day of Refreshing" retreat sponsored by Psalm One Ministries conducted by Linda Kline, the Pastoral Director. For more information about this ministry please log on to www.psalmone.org.

"Life in the slow lane" this awakening expression, was almost foreign to me. Much of my life had been spent living in the fast lane. Multi-tasking was the norm. I constantly functioned out of a state of hurriedness. My days and many evenings were filled with activity.

Despite my busyness, there was always an internal longing for more of the pleasures of tranquility. It was a heart cry that I rarely articulated. God, however, was listening attentively to the rapid beats of my heart. He was leading me to those tranquil pathways. He was leading me to live my life at a much different pace.

Reflections of the Journey:

1. What does the current pace of your life look like? Slow, moderate, fast, or out of control?

_____

_____

_____

_____

_____

_____

_____

_____

2. What steps can you take to reach more tranquil pathways? What would tranquil pathways look like to you?

_____

_____

_____

_____

_____

_____

_____

_____

_____

Prayer for the Journey:

_____

_____

_____

_____

_____

_____

_____

_____

_____

_____

10

Rhythms of the Heart

"He leads me beside still waters." Psalm 23:2

The heart is a muscle that pumps blood through the blood vessels by way of repeated, rhythmic contractions. The normal adult heart rate is about 70 to 80 beats per minute.

Heartbeats originate in the heart's pacemaker by way of electrical signals. The heart rate is determined by the rate in which the pacemaker discharges the electrical signals. An abnormal heart rhythm means the heart is beating too fast or too slow.

The heart is also the center of our being. From that innermost place come our thoughts, inclinations, reflections, our consciences, our appetites, our emotions. It is the soul. While the rhythm of our physical heart may be normal, the rhythms of our souls are abnormal. Abnormalities in the realm of the soul can present themselves in various forms, including anxiety, bitterness, or faintheartedness.

How does our heart (our life) get out of rhythm, moving too quickly or too slowly? The experiences, circumstances, and trials of life can result in abnormal heart rhythms. Our own striving can cause abnormal heart rhythms. We can get out of rhythm with God when we try to live our lives in our own strength. We can get out of rhythm when we allow others to determine our priorities, set our schedules, or dictate our pace. We are out of rhythm when we lag behind. We are out of rhythm when we walk in disobedience. We are out of rhythm when we are outside of His will. But, because of God's great compassion, as the Great Shepherd, He will lead us into times of refreshing and restore our souls to normal rhythms.

Reflections of the Journey:

1. How would you rate your current heart (soul) rhythms? Are you experiencing anxiety, bitterness, or faintheartedness?

_____

_____

_____

_____

_____

_____

_____

2. What steps could you take to return your soul to more normal rhythms?

_____

_____

_____

_____

_____

_____

_____

Prayer for the Journey:

_____

_____

_____

_____

_____

_____

_____

_____

_____

_____

11

Following the Shepherd

"Then you will understand what is right and just and fair – every good path." Proverbs 2:9, NIV

The Lord wants to shepherd us. It is an emphatic fact that streams throughout biblical history. As a demonstration of His commitment to it, He laid down His life (see John 10:11).

As Shepherd, He strengthens the weak, heals the sick, binds up the injured, brings back the strays, and searches for the lost. He calls, He guides, and He speaks. "The Lord is my shepherd, I shall not want" (Psalm 23:1) is the opening declaration from a young shepherd, musician, poet, military commander, king, prophet, and worshipper of the Most High God. It is a statement of assurance and comfort from an experienced follower. Knowing Him as Shepherd, David goes on to say, "He makes me lie down in green pastures; He leads me beside still waters. He restores my soul" (verses 2-3). This portion of the much beloved 23rd Psalm expresses the great care the Shepherd has for the sheep of His pasture.

When we are in a spiritual desert, as a result of our circumstances, or because we are out of rhythm with God, or both, it is the Shepherd who leads us to the pastures of His Divine providence. When we are weary and overwhelmed, and our soul is cast down, it is the Shepherd who leads us to the quiet streams of restoration.

Affliction lends opportunity for the Holy Spirit to reveal any rhythmic abnormalities. That revelation lends opportunity for spiritual transformation. Spiritual transformation allows us to learn of His ways. His ways are righteous. And isn't that the goal of every believer, to reflect the righteousness of God in all that we do? Yes would be the answer to this question. Without the Shepherd's guidance, however, it is impossible to learn His ways and to reflect His righteousness.

The Psalmist was aware of this truth and he goes on to say, "He leads me in the paths of righteousness for his name's sake" (verse 3). Can't you hear the Shepherd calling? "Come this way. Follow Me. Keep the covenant. Then you will learn that my ways are "loving and faithful" (see Psalm 25:10, NIV); "Then you will understand what is right and just and fair – every good path" (Proverbs 2:9, NIV).

Could it be that our *broken-wing* is a tool in the hand of God to help us recognize that we are out of rhythm, and of how desperately we need the green pastures, the still waters, and guidance in the paths of righteousness?

When the world around you looks dry, the doctor's report is negative, more treatment than anticipated is required, the diagnosis turned out to be wrong, the pain has not subsided, and the end does not seem to be near, just keep following the Shepherd. Go lie in the green pastures and sit beside the quiet streams. Listen and learn His ways. The Shepherd wants the rhythm of your heart to synchronize with His own.

Reflections of the Journey:

1. How has God used your broken-wing to help you recognize that your life may be out of rhythm?

_____

_____

_____

_____

_____

_____

_____

_____

2. What "green pastures" and "quiet streams" are currently available to you? If none, can you create some for yourself? What would they be?

_____

_____

_____

_____

_____

_____

_____

_____

_____

Prayer for the Journey:

_____

_____

_____

_____

_____

_____

_____

_____

_____

_____

12

The Blessing of Waiting

"I waited patiently for the LORD; and He inclined to me and heard my cry." Psalm 40:1, NASB

Life in the slow lane is to live our appointed days at an unhurried pace. Life in the slow lane provides us with the opportunity to apprehend the blessings of waiting. Waiting requires that we trust God. Waiting tests our faith. Waiting takes time.

All time is governed by God (see Daniel 2:21). We often think of time in increments of days, weeks, months, and years. But within the progression of chronological time, God utilizes set or appointed times. We see this throughout biblical history. God used set and appointed times to reveal His mysteries (see Ephesians 1:9-10), to send forth His Son (see Galatians 4:4), to announce the coming of the kingdom of God (see Mark 1:15), and to release His word (see Titus 1:1-3).

God also uses set or appointed times for our deliverance. While we are waiting, He uses the chronological time to perfect His purposes in our lives. Transformation is evident in the person who has learned to wait. David was one of those persons and reveals the blessing of waiting in the first few verses of Psalm 40:1-4:

"I waited patiently for the LORD; And He inclined to me and heard my cry. He brought me up out of the pit of destruction, out of the miry clay, And He set my feet upon a rock making my footsteps firm. He put a new song in my mouth, a song of praise to our God; Many will see and fear And will trust in the LORD. How blessed is the man who has made the LORD his trust, And has not turned to the proud, nor to those who lapse into falsehood." (NASB)

The list of blessings David received included deliverance, a firm spiritual foundation, and a new song of praise to God. Finally, David's waiting is a testimony that encourages others to put their trust in God alone.

Waiting must be active and relevant, not passive and meaningless. Active and relevant waiting means being faithful to God in all things. I liken active waiting to the farmer who is waiting for his crops to break above the soil's surface. The farmer has tilled the soil; he has sown seen in the ground; and he tends the land, watching for and eliminating weeds, etc. Now he must wait. As he waits for the land to yield its crops, he must be patient and steadfast. He must not give up when there are no visible signs of productivity.

A few years ago, I had a memorable dream. In it, the Lord led me out to an open field, and as far as I could see there was what seemed like acres of black dirt. As I looked out, I saw nothing peeking above the ground – no crops. From what I could see, it was barren. The Lord spoke, "Put your hand under the dirt." At the Lord's bidding, I reached up under the dirt and pulled out three pieces of wheat. Afterwards the Lord spoke again, "See, I told you something was out here." At that point the dream ended. This symbolic dream, one I have recalled on numerous occasions, serves as a reminder to remain faithful in waiting. Our *broken-wing* may make life seem barren, but at the appointed time new life will spring forth. If we remain committed to the Lord, regardless of the obstacles we may be facing at the moment, there will be a spiritual harvest.

James, although referring to the second coming of Christ, says this: "Be patient, therefore, brothers, until the coming of the Lord. See how the farmer waits for the precious fruit of the earth, being patient about it, until it receives the early and the late rains" (James 5:7).

As I have waited for healing, I have been blessed with much. I have been greatly encouraged by the testimony of David, but the greater blessing has been seeing God at work through my own experience.

Reflections of the Journey:

1. Name times in your life when it has been evident that what took place occurred at God's appointed times.

_____

_____

_____

_____

_____

2. List how you have been blessed in the waiting.

_____

_____

_____

_____

_____

_____

_____

_____

Prayer for the Journey:

_____

_____

_____

_____

_____

_____

_____

_____

_____

_____

13

An Expected End

"For as the heavens are higher than the earth, so are my ways higher than your ways and my thoughts than your thoughts." Isaiah 55:9

Life in the slow lane can sometimes lead us on paths that seem peculiar, uncertain, and never ending, but we must maintain our hope. For all of us, there is an expected end.

About three years into my journey, the Lord gave me a promise found in Psalm 71:20-21:

"Though you have made me see troubles, many and bitter, you will restore my life again; from the depths of the earth you will again bring me up. You will increase my honor and comfort me once again" (NIV).

I have yet to understand how this specifically applies to my life. I am unaware of what God has defined as restoration, honor, and comfort because I do not know what is in His mind. But when I read and meditate on this passage, I am filled with hope. There is one thing I am certain of. He will fulfill what He has promised in His Word. I often reflect on the words of the Lord spoken through Isaiah:

"For as the heavens are higher than the earth, so are my ways higher than your ways and my thoughts than your thoughts. For as the rain and the snow come down from heaven and do not return there but water the earth, making it bring forth and sprout, giving seed to the sower and bread to the eater, so shall my word be that goes out from my mouth; it shall not return to me empty, but it shall accomplish that which I purpose, and shall succeed in the thing for which I sent it" (Isaiah 55:9-11).

While I wait for the Word to produce the harvest God has planned, I am being blessed. I am enjoying the green pastures and the quiet streams. I am endeavoring to follow the Shepherd as He gets my heart in rhythm. He is leading me to His expected end.

You may think of your affliction as an annoying disruption to your pace, but reconsider your thoughts. Is God telling you to Stop! Wait! Slow down! and experience life in the slow lane?

Are you willing to follow the Shepherd? Are you willing to let Him adjust the rhythms of your heart? If you answered yes to these questions, take comfort, knowing that the Lord, the Great Shepherd, will lead you to His expected end.

Reflections of the Journey:

1. Write out promises from God's word that sustain and comfort you while you await your expected end.

_____

_____

_____

_____

_____

_____

_____

2. Explain how you may have seen your affliction as an annoying disruption. How can you turn your thoughts around to see the blessings God has for you in the waiting?

_____

_____

_____

_____

_____

_____

_____

Prayer for the Journey:

_____

_____

_____

_____

_____

_____

_____

_____

_____

_____

_____

14

The Sufficiency of His Grace

"Yours, O LORD, is the greatness and the power and the glory and the victory and the majesty, for all that is in the heavens and in the earth is yours. Yours is the kingdom, O LORD, and you are exalted as head above all." 1 Chronicles 29:11

Grace…the silent wonder of His unmerited favor. Grace…the abundant gift of a loving Savior. Grace…the power and strength that bears the weaknesses of the flesh. Grace…the foundation of endurance. Grace…it's what causes us to triumph, even when we have a *broken-wing*.

The day had been long; the discomfort from this neurological disorder had been agonizing. I was weary and wondered when this season of suffering would cease. As streams of tears ran down my face, I scribbled on a piece of paper, "His grace is sufficient for me." Writing down those six words was a pivotal moment. It would be the commencement of a personal revelation of what it meant to live in the sufficiency of His grace while suffering from a *broken-wing*. Little did I know that my seemingly darkened world was about to be illuminated.

When I think of grace, I often think of the Apostle Paul. In the third heaven, Paul heard revelations that were so astounding that he was not permitted to speak about them. It was his " in the body or out of the body" (2 Corinthians 12:3) experience that led to him being given "a thorn in his flesh." He was tormented by it, but it was given to keep him from becoming conceited (see 2 Corinthians 12:7). Three times the Apostle pleaded with the Lord for its removal, but the Lord's response was far different from Paul's petition:

"But he said to me, 'My grace is sufficient for you, for my power is made perfect in weakness.' Therefore I will boast all the more gladly of my weaknesses, so that the power of Christ may rest upon me." (2 Corinthians 12:9).

Paul's post-paradise revelation could be summarized in this statement: Our weakness is the Lord's ally and our strength is His opponent. Paul's weakness created the opening for the Lord's power to rest upon him. The Lord's power would dwell within him and operate through him to boldly proclaim the gospel, to perform numerous signs and wonders, to win souls for the kingdom of God, to instruct, to correct, and to build up the faith of the believers.

The words of the Lord recorded in the ancient text weren't merely a portion of a letter written to the church at Corinth. They have resounding present-day relevance. As I mediated on the passage, I was awakened by its truth, and invigorating joy filled my heart.

I began to emerge from the shadow of my *broken-wing* and focus on God's brilliant transcendence, for He is above all, greater than all, more powerful than all. I began to focus on the immenseness of His strength and prayed for a portion of it to become my own. Everything I needed for this journey was within Him.

When the Apostle Paul recounted His vision of fourteen years prior, I am sure he had no idea of the impact it would have in the centuries to come. There would be multitudes of people after him would walk under the tabernacle of sufficient grace. By God's grace, they would tread through the valleys of affliction and find strength in the weaknesses caused by their *broken-wing*. By His grace, they would forge forward to pursue life, to survive, and to discover and fulfill their God-given purpose and destiny.

Reflections of the Journey:

1. What is your understanding of grace?

_____

_____

_____

_____

_____

_____

2. Can you with joy and assurance quote 2 Corinthians 12:9 and make it your own? Here it is as a reminder: "But he said to me, 'My grace is sufficient for you, for my power is made perfect in weakness.' Therefore I will boast all the more gladly of my weaknesses, so that the power of Christ may rest upon me." Consider writing out this verse and keeping it handy.

_____

_____

_____

_____

_____

_____

_____

Prayer for the Journey:

_____

_____

_____

_____

_____

_____

_____

_____

_____

_____

15

Images of Grace

"But Jesus looked at them and said, 'With man this is impossible, but with God all things are possible.' " Matthew 19:26

The nostalgic photography of Gordon Parks, the folk-style paintings of Clementine Hunter, the expressionism and primitivism in the paintings of William Henry Johnson, and the realism in the paintings of Henry Ossawa Tanner are their artistic creative images of life. Images capture a moment. They make visible what has been seen.

On my journey I encountered many images. The encounters were unexpected and brief, but the message was impactful. I did not photograph them or duplicate them on canvas, wood, or paper. I captured them in my mind. They would become the touchstones to help keep me on the path. If they could be considered a valuable artistic collection, I would call them "Images of Grace."

Why images of grace? Because they captured a moment in time when God seemed to be saying, "They have made it by walking in the abundance of my grace and so can you." Each of them had a *broken-wing* and had been on the journey through affliction for a very long time.

The first encounter was at a leadership summit. I saw the fortitude of a gifted musician whose physical challenges did not prevent him from playing in a marching band, singing, and strumming up wonderful sonatas on the black and white keys of a piano. I watched in utter amazement as he utilized his musical gifts with precision and confidence.

A second encounter came as I awoke from a late afternoon nap just in time to see a television broadcast featuring a quadriplegic woman. In her self-narrative, she discussed the drastic lifestyle adjustments following a traumatic accident. Her global ministry has blessed numerous individuals whose lives have been adversely impacted by disabilities. I consider her faith in God, strength, determination, and long-standing commitment to be phenomenal.

By far, the encounter that had the greatest impact occurred one Sunday afternoon, while attending a festival in Eaton, Ohio, northwest of my home. I met a young mother, partially paralyzed. As we briefly chatted, she voluntarily explained that she had suffered two strokes. She referred to the deadness in the right side of her body. She pulled up her sleeves, comparing the weakness and thinness of her right arm with the strength and taut muscular form of her left. She further expounded on how she had to use her left arm to compensate for what she was unable to do with her right arm. During our conversation, I also observed that her right leg was in a brace that obviously provided mobility assistance. "I used to get upset about it," she went on to say, "but not any longer."

I did not ask her to elaborate on how or when she reached the point of being able to propel beyond the mental and emotional anguish of dealing with a *broken-wing*. I simply captured the brief moments in her presence as yet another encouraging lesson in overcoming obstacles.

Our conversation ended and she went on her way. Her joyful demeanor, glowing smile, and upbeat attitude left an impression that I will always remember.

The physically disabled musician, the heroic quadriplegic ambassador, and the partially paralyzed young women – they are all memorable images. Whenever I recall their stories, I summarize them in six words: God's grace is more than enough.

God's grace abounds in the lives of those who are suffering with a *broken-wing* of any type. His power overshadows the weakness of our flesh. To see His grace in action, we must be yielded vessels, willing to look beyond limitations and seek God's face for the possibilities.

Reflections of the Journey:

1. What individuals can you hold up as examples of those who are adversely impacted by disabilities, but who show a willingness to look beyond their limitations and seek God's face for possibilities?

_____

_____

_____

_____

_____

2. As you continue on your journey of affliction, can you embrace the following words: "God's grace is more than enough"?

_____

_____

_____

_____

Prayer for the Journey:

_____

_____

_____

_____

_____

_____

_____

_____

_____

_____

16

A Treasure in Your Earthen Vessel

"But we have this treasure in earthen vessels, so that the surpassing greatness of the power will be of God and not from ourselves." 2 Corinthians 4:7, NASB

Like vessels of clay, we are fragile and easily broken. We are all subject to human weaknesses, yet God chooses to shine through us to reveal His glory. The "surpassing power" of God is so great and the light is so bright that it is in no way hindered by the fragileness of the clay. His power transcends all of mortality.

Your life is a testimony to the grace of a loving Savior. There is a treasure in your earthen vessel. You were created to be a light. Turning to Christ put you in a unique position to reflect His radiance. By the power of His Spirit, you are not only being progressively transformed into His likeness, but also "you will shine among them like stars in the sky as you hold firmly to the word of life" (see Philippians 2:15-16, NIV).

Jesus declared in His Sermon on the Mount:

"You are the light of the world. A city set on a hill cannot be hidden. Nor do people light a lamp and put it under a basket, but on a stand, and it gives light to all in the house. In the same way, let your light shine before others, so that they may see your good works and give glory to your Father who is in heaven" (Matthew 5:14-16).

Now, declare these words over your life:

- I am not discounted because of my physical weakness.

- My *broken-wing* is a platform for His greatness.

- Through His strength and power, I will forge forward to pursue the life He has for me.

- Because of Christ, I am a light for His glory.

- Daily, I am walking in the abundance of His grace.

Reflections of the Journey:

1. Do you see your life as a testimony to the grace of a loving Savior? If so, elaborate. If not, what will it take for you to be able to embrace the words above?

_____

_____

_____

_____

_____

_____

_____

2. Take time every day, preferably early in the day, to recite and declare over yourself the statements that completed today's reading.

_____

_____

_____

_____

_____

Prayer for the Journey:

_____

_____

_____

_____

_____

_____

_____

_____

_____

_____

_____

_____

_____

17

Pursuing God Through Prayer

"Whom have I in heaven but you? And there is nothing on earth that I desire besides you. My flesh and my heart may fail, but God is the strength of my heart and my portion forever."
Psalm 73:25-26

Prayer and worship have been essential for my spiritual journey. They have been my source for communing with God – the only One who can satisfy my deepest thirsts and greatest hunger.

Living with a *broken-wing* has led me to view both disciplines from a uniquely different perspective. Prayer and worship had to be more than the spoken words and the outward expressions. Thus, another part of the journey began as I pursued God through prayer.

"Let my prayer be counted as incense before you, and the lifting up of my hands as the evening sacrifice!" (Psalm 141:2)

A bright-green Huffy two-wheeler bicycle; the white house with green shutters; the big maroon Buick that transported us about town to places such as the airport where my dad played baseball and to Sunday morning church services; the navy blue Ford Galaxy 500 (our first new car). They are all remnants that remind me of my childhood. Outside of the warm memories, they had no lasting value and are no longer a part of my life. There is, however, one particular childhood memory that has lingered through the years. It has eternal value and remains an integral part of my life. It is prayer.

Table blessings and simple bedtime prayers were the foundation of my prayer life. In our home, it was imperative that I not dive into one of my mother's scrumptious southern-style meals or lay my head upon my pillow to rest without first offering up a prayer. Forgetting to pray would result in a gentle rebuke or a glance of displeasure. As a very young child, I sensed through my mother's teaching that there was great value in what I later learned would be conversation, journaling, contemplation, and intercession.

Prayer is sacred communion with God, as we offer our praise and thanksgiving. And it's the avenue by which we present our petitions. Prayer should be an unceasing daily activity. Through prayer, lives are saved. Through prayer, we are spiritually transformed. Through prayer, we hear and are admonished to respond to the Holy Spirit's leading. Prayerful meditation on the Word, another form of prayer, will unlock its truths and teach us about the character of God and how to apply the Word to our lives. God responds to heartfelt prayer with mercy, grace, peace, comfort, direction, and deliverance.

Prayer is a journey. In the infant stages of my prayer life, I often stumbled through the sacred exercise. I struggled with what words to say, repetitive phrases, length, and volume. I heard and put into practice all types of formulas for prayer. I flailed about trying to quiet all of the rumblings and chatter in my soul and focus on communing with God. I tried, failed, and tried again. Despite the difficulties of the prayer journey, I was determined to forge ahead in my pursuit.

Reflections of the Journey:

1. What part does prayer currently play in your life?

_____

_____

_____

_____

_____

_____

_____

_____

_____

2. What steps might you take to set aside time to pray more consistently?

_____

_____

_____

_____

_____

_____

_____

_____

_____

_____

Prayer for the Journey:

_____

_____

_____

_____

_____

_____

_____

_____

_____

_____

18

Allowing My Heart to Speak

"Then they arose early in the morning and worshiped before the Lord, and returned again to their house in Ramah. And Elkanah had relations with Hannah his wife, and the Lord remembered her. It came about in due time, after Hannah had conceived, that she gave birth to a son; and she named him Samuel, saying 'Because I have asked him of the Lord." 1 Samuel 1:19-20, NASB

To some degree, our prayer lives are shaped by our environment. Throughout the development of my Christian faith, I listened attentively to the eloquent orations of preachers who prayed so fervently. Their voices echoed loudly and their prayers seemed to electrify the atmosphere. I thought that I needed to mimic that same style to assure that my prayers reached God…so I did. I also heard prayers that were scripted and almost anticipated what was going to be said next. I found myself repeating some of the same scripted phrases too, believing that without them my prayers were incomplete. It was all a learning process. It was the words of Christ, however, as He taught the multitudes on the mountainside that offered me some truth about the discipline of prayer:

"When you pray, you are not to be like the hypocrites; for they love to stand and pray in the synagogues and on the street corners so that they may be seen by men. Truly I say to you, they have their reward in full. But you, when you pray, go into your inner room, close your door and pray to your Father who is in secret, and your Father who sees what is done in secret will reward you. And when you are praying, do not use meaningless repetition as the Gentiles do, for they suppose that they will be heard for their many words. So do not be like them; for your Father knows what you need before you ask Him" (Matthew 6:5-8, NASB).

Prayer is beyond what is spoken. Whether the words are as articulate as the poignant words of the psalmist or just short simple phrases, it's the intent of the heart that punctuates its sincerity. The major goal of all prayer is that we will meet with our Holy God. In one of David's psalms of praise is this promise about prayer:

"The LORD is near to all who call on him, to all who call on him in truth" (Psalm 145:18).

Life experiences can totally revolutionize our prayer lives. Living with a *broken-wing* changed mine. I longed to pray aloud without debilitating pain. I was desperate for God to hear my audible prayers, so I would often push to my physical extremity, but the pain and involuntary muscle contractions soon reminded me of the need to silence my voice. When I would push beyond my physical capabilities, it would often take days for my system to recover.

My frustration over this lingering season of affliction forced me to ask God: "How can I commune with You, intercede for others, and offer up prayers of petition if I cannot communicate effectively?" God responded to my inner cries and led me to the first book of Samuel. It was in that Old Testament text that I found great comfort as I read the story of Hannah.

Hannah, barren, one of the wives of Elkanah, poured out her heart to God for a son at the temple in Shiloh:

"She, greatly distressed, prayed to the Lord and wept bitterly. She made a vow and said, 'O Lord of hosts, if You will indeed look on the affliction of Your maidservant and remember me, and not forget Your maidservant, but will give Your maidservant a son, then I will give him to the Lord all the days of his life, and a razor shall never come on his head.' Now it came about, as she continued praying before the Lord, that Eli was watching her mouth. As for Hannah, she was speaking in her heart, only her lips were moving, but her voice was not heard. So Eli thought she was drunk. Then Eli said to her, 'How long will you make yourself drunk? Put away your wine from you.' But Hannah replied, 'No, my lord, I am a woman oppressed in spirit; I have drunk neither wine nor strong drink, but I have poured out my soul before the Lord. Do not consider your maidservant as a worthless woman, for I have spoken until now out of my great concern and provocation.' Then Eli answered and said, 'Go in peace; and may the God of Israel grant your petition that you have asked of Him.' She said, 'Let your maidservant find favor in your sight.' So the woman went her way and ate, and her face was no longer sad" (1 Samuel 1:10-18, NASB).

"As for Hannah, she was speaking in her heart" (verse 13); it was this portion of the biblical narrative that caused my heart to leap. This powerful revelation in God's Word put an end to my internal struggle regarding prayer. Through Hannah's story, God was saying that prayers need not be audible to be effective. To Eli, the priest in Shiloh, Hannah appeared to be drunk, but to God it was the fragrant incense of secret prayers of the heart. God responded to the cries of Hannah's heart and granted her request.

Hannah's story changed my view of prayer. Yes, God loves to hear the audible expressions of prayer. However, when I cannot verbalize my prayers, I simple allow my heart to speak.

Reflections of the Journey:

1. In what ways might your current affliction hinder your prayers?

_____

_____

_____

_____

_____

_____

_____

_____

_____

2. How does it make you feel to know that God responded to the cries of Hannah's heart and granted her request and that He will listen to your heart's cry as well?

_____

_____

_____

_____

_____

_____

_____

Prayer for the Journey:

_____

_____

_____

_____

_____

_____

_____

_____

_____

_____

_____

19

Pursuing the Heart of God Through Worship

"One thing have I asked of the LORD, that will I seek after: that I may dwell in the house of the LORD all the days of my life, to gaze upon the beauty of the LORD and to inquire in his temple." Psalm 27:4

"Purify my worship, oh, God," became my unceasing prayer. I was not satisfied with litanies, liturgies, or lyrics. And while I loved participating in all of the forms of worship, I would not be satisfied until I had in earnestness touch His heart.

Pursuing the heart of God through worship – for me – is to reach a place where I am in sacred Spirit-to-spirit communion with God. It's where the world and all of my adversities fade into the background. It's the place where my mind is focused solely on the King of all glory.

Worship is to give reverence to God for all that He is. It is the human response to His grace, loving-kindness, faithfulness, sovereignty, righteousness, and truth. It is adoration, praise, and thanksgiving. It is the human acknowledgement of Him as the Creator, Sovereign Ruler, and Sustainer of the Universe. To worship is to serve, offering our bodies sacrificially. Worship is the perpetual stream that flows out of our relationship with God.

According to the Word of God, worship is commanded. On the majestic smoke-covered mountain called Mount Sinai, Moses was given the law. Etched in the stone were these words:

"And God spoke all these words, saying, 'I am the LORD your God, who brought you out of the land of Egypt, out of the house of slavery. You shall have no other gods before me. You shall not make for yourself a carved image, or any likeness of anything that is in heaven above, or that is in the earth beneath, or that is in the water under the earth. You shall not bow down to them or serve them, for I the LORD your God am a jealous God, visiting the iniquity of the fathers on the children to the third and the fourth generation of those who hate me, but showing steadfast love to thousands of those who love me and keep my commandments' " (Exodus 20:1-6).

The Psalms, for example, are replete with calls to worship the Lord:

"Ascribe to the Lord, O mighty ones, ascribe to the Lord glory and strength. Ascribe to the Lord the glory due his name; worship the Lord in the splendor of his holiness" (Psalm 29:1-2, NIV).

In the wilderness, the Messiah thwarts Satan's wiles to gain worship for himself:

"And the devil took him up and showed him all the kingdoms of the world in a moment of time, and said to him, 'To you I will give all this authority and their glory, for it has been delivered to me, and I give it to whom I will. If you, then, will worship me, it will all be yours.' And Jesus answered him, 'It is written, You shall worship the Lord your God, and him only shall you serve'" (Luke 4:5-8).

The worship of God is commanded, but it also has an expression. It is to be expressed through our life-style. It is also expressed privately and corporately through verbal declarations, singing, bowing, the clapping of hands, dancing, the playing of instruments, or through service. Either way, it must have deep roots and a firm foundation.

Jesus would clarify this in His conversation with the Samaritan woman at Jacob's well in a town called Sychar:

" 'Our fathers worshiped on this mountain, but you say that in Jerusalem is the place where people ought to worship.' Jesus said to her, 'Woman, believe me, the hour is coming when neither on this mountain nor in Jerusalem will you worship the Father' " (John 4:20-21).

Neither Mount Gerizim nor Jerusalem define worship that pleases God. Worship is not about a place. Religious formalities do not define true worship of the Father. The volume of our worship does not dictate its depth.

Our reverencing Him, regardless of the expression, must find its roots deep within our hearts. God, who "Sits enthroned upon the cherubim" (Psalm 99:1) seeks adoration, praise, and thanksgiving that stand on the foundation of sincerity. Jesus goes on to say to the Samaritan woman, who was in desperate need of and received a revelation:

"But the hour is coming, and is now here, when the true worshipers will worship the Father in spirit and truth, for the Father is seeking such people to worship him. God is spirit, and those who worship him must worship in spirit and truth" (John 4:23-24).

Reflections of the Journey:

1. What is your understanding of worship and how and when do you express your worship unto the Lord?

_____

_____

_____

2. What steps might you take to enhance your worship?

_____

_____

_____

_____

_____

Prayer for the Journey:

_____

_____

_____

_____

_____

_____

_____

_____

_____

_____

_____

20

A Personal Experience with Worship

"I will bless the Lord at all times; his praise shall continually be in my mouth. My soul makes its boast in the Lord; let the humble hear and be glad. Oh magnify the Lord with me, and let us exalt his name together." Psalm 34:1-3

Our experiences with worship are vast. Worship as I knew it in the early days of my Christian journey was primarily related to music. I grew up learning hymns, singing spirituals and what is often termed as "gospel music."

As a young child, I distinctly remember laying my head on my mother's chest just to hear the vibrations of her soft, high-pitched soprano voice as she sang along with the congregation during Sunday morning services. What a glorious sound! It was evident that she not only enjoyed what she was singing, but also she was singing from her heart. The sound brought a calm that flooded my heart as I drifted off to sleep. As I grew older, sleeping during church services was out of the question – a thump on the head served as a reminder.

During the season of my physical affliction, my oral expressions of worship were rarely punctuated with such reverberating sounds. When I sang or made declarative statements of adoration to my God, it was often in the form of intermittent syllables. This raised some questions. "How can I worship You in Spirit and in truth when dealing with such pain, a locked jaw, and limited speech?" "How do I touch Your heart?" My continued pursuit of Him would soon reveal the answer to these questions.

While waiting for a response, I thought, "I have to keep trying." Thus, like I did in prayer, I often pushed beyond my physical abilities because I felt it demonstrated perseverance. I somehow had the notion that without audible and visible expressions, my worship was not God-honoring.

It was in the corporate setting where I felt the greatest anxiety. "What will people think of me if I am not participating in corporate worship with the same fervor as the rest of the assembly of God's people? Why it may appear that I have no faith and am giving into this horrid infirmity!" Through God, I would later recognize that these types of thoughts – though quite real – are nothing more than bondage.

One Sunday things changed. The forceful contractions in my jaw and head on that particular morning were agonizing. Yet I had such a desire to openly verbalize my adoration for God. The physical anguish, however, was more than I could bear for the moment, so I silenced my voice. Feelings of defeat began to flood my mind. Sensing the anguish in my soul, God gently whispered, "I'm looking at your heart." At that moment, I felt a freedom that I had not known. I was no longer bound by thoughts of defeat and inadequacy.

I was at peace, knowing that my outward expressions of worship were not nearly as important as the source from whence they came. God was listening to the internal vibrations; He was listening for sincerity. That's the sound that reaches heaven. That's the sound that touches the heart of God. That's the sound of true worship.

Like the Samaritan woman at Jacob's well, I had had an encounter. The hour had come and this fresh very personal revelation of truth revolutionized both my private and corporate worship.

Final Words for the Journey

A life of intimacy with God is for all of us. He wants to be our God. Our innate desire is to be at one with him. We should not allow our *broken-wing* to prevent us from worshipping a most Holy God nor should we allow it to extinguish the flame of fellowship found in prayer.

Volume, length, verbiage, and voice fluctuations do not, my dear friends, determine whether or not God hears and is honored by our worship or moved by our prayers. God is touched by the secret prayers and the internal vibrations of a sincere heart.

Reflections of the Journey:

1. If your affliction stands in the way of how you would like to worship or serve the Lord, do you ever find yourself concerned about what others might think? How do you deal with those feelings?

_____

_____

_____

_____

2. Has something happened in your life that has served to reveal to you a personal truth that, in turn, has revolutionized your private and corporate worship? Explain.

_____

_____

_____

Prayer for the Journey:

_____

_____

_____

_____

_____

_____

_____

_____

_____

_____

_____

_____

_____

_____

_____

21

Behold the Creator

"For this reason I bow my knees before the Father, from whom every family in heaven and on earth is named, that according to the riches of his glory he may grant you to be strengthened with power through his Spirit in your inner being, so that Christ may dwell in your hearts through faith – that you, being rooted and grounded in love, may have strength to comprehend with all the saints what is the breadth and length and height and depth, and to know the love of Christ that surpasses knowledge, that you may be filled with all the fullness of God." Ephesians 3:14-19

The greatness of God is revealed through every creature of the great sea, every winged bird that flies above the earth's surface in the open expanse of heaven, all cattle, every insect, reptile, and through every beast that moves about the earth.

As Moses concludes the narrative of the fifth day of creation, he writes "And God saw that it was good" (see Genesis 1:20-25.) Thus all that God created, like God Himself, is perfect.

Many species of birds were created on that day. Among them was the popular Bald Eagle. With its radiant white crown and tail feathers, it is a majestic symbol of beauty and strength. Its swiftness is remarkable, moving at speeds of approximately 44 miles-per-hour when gliding and up to 100 miles-per-hour when diving. God fashioned the wings of eagles in such a way that they are able to soar on the wind at incredible heights of up to 10,000 feet above the earth's surface. They are marvelous creatures, representing one of the many portraits of God's perfection.

Since the beginning of time, God has revealed "His invisible attributes, His eternal power and divine nature" (see Romans 1:20, NASB) through all that He spoke into existence.

Throughout the written Word of God, we find narratives, poetic expressions, hymns of praise, and prophecy which contain imageries of God at work in nature: the firmament in full array with its splendid sunrises and colorful sunsets, the intense white light of the moon governing the night sky, every star in its place and accounted for, the displays of natural wonders, the water, the wind, and the activity of the creatures of the air, land, and sea.

These various imageries of nature speak of the power, majesty, character, and glory of God the Creator. From them we learn many spiritual truths that become fuel for our pilgrimage on the earth.

In Babylon, where Isaiah delivered the message of comfort to the exiled nation, he tells them that if they would wait on the Lord – place all of their hope in Him – their strength would be renewed and their spiritual power increased. They would be exalted to great spiritual heights (see Isaiah 40:29-31). In this passage, it is the eagle who takes center stage. The Creator through the creature has a vital message.

Reflections of the Journey:

1. What in nature speaks to you of the power, majesty, character, and glory of God?

_____

_____

_____

_____

_____

_____

_____

_____

2. As God spoke to the exiled nations, He speaks to us today and says that if we wait our strength will be renewed and our spiritual power will be increased. Describe what you think it means to have your strength renewed and your spiritual power increased.

_____

_____

_____

_____

_____

_____

_____

_____

_____

_____

Prayer for the Journey:

_____

_____

_____

_____

_____

_____

_____

_____

_____

_____

_____

22

Kingston's Story
– A Parable

"Yet I will rejoice in the Lord; I will take joy in the God of my salvation. God, the Lord is my strength; he makes my feet like the deer's; he makes me tread on my high places." Habakkuk 3:18-19

The day broke forth with the eastern rising of the sun. Its warmth was soothing as it cut through the brisk air of the morning. The dew in the field beneath his feet sparkled as its moisture caressed his ankles.

Kingston began each of his days out in the field gazing at the mountainous landscape toward the west. Several miles away was a place he liked to call "Homestead." As the birds chirped, his mind carried him to years prior when he dwelled in Homestead. He remembered the activities he used to participate in, the laughter, the work he once did in the marketplace. He remembered the freedom. But it had all changed one day after an almost tragic event altered his life. He was now residing in a place called Strangeland.

He hoped to return to Homestead, but he did not know when or how. He wondered if he would ever recapture the life he had known before. "Only God knows," he thought to himself. Feeling weary from the weight of his journey, he knelt in the field. Tears began to flow as he poured out his heart before the Lord. "Father," he prayed, "my hope is fading. I want to be well again. I want to be restored. I want to return to Homestead, but it seems as though it's never going to happen. Where do I turn now? What is the next step? How can I survive?"

Suddenly in the distance he heard a rustling in the grass. He opened his eyes and just as he began to rise from his knees, a Herald showed up. "Good morning, sir. I heard that you were longing for Homestead."

"Yes," the weary Kingston replied, "I am."

"Well, I have a message for you." He handed him a silver envelope with a red seal on the outside. Kingston's heart leaped as he anticipated its contents.

"Who is this from?" asked Kingston. But when he looked up, the Herald was gone. Kingston broke the red seal and proceeded to open the envelope. Inside was a letter:

Dear Kingston:

I know you have a broken-wing and have been in much distress about your physical challenges and your sojourn in Strangeland. I also know that you are putting all of your hope in being restored to what once was. I can certainly do that, for it is within my power to do so. But I want to teach you to put all of your hope in me. The strength that you need to endure this season is found only in me. If you totally trust me, you will find rest for your weary soul. If you totally trust me, you will discover that you will rise to spiritual heights higher than the mountains that stand before you. You see, son, you were destined to soar. Signed Adonai

Kingston folded the letter, placed it back in the envelope, and began his short journey back to Strangeland. As he knelt to pray that night, etched in his mind was his early morning encounter with the Herald.

The next morning he returned to the field where once again he gazed at the mountainous landscape ahead of him and began to weep. "I feel so alone," he thought. "I can't seem to find comfort; I need to be restored. Adonai," he cried out. "I need you!"

Suddenly, a strong wind began to blow across the field. Nearby, trees began to bend as the wind forced them from their erect positions. Flower petals whirled through the air. Water from a nearby pond began to splash up on the grassy shores. Kingston braced himself against a huge rock to shield himself from the gusts of the wind. He closed his eyes and cried out again, "Adonai, I need you!"

As quickly as the words left his lips, he felt the wind lift him until he reached an altitude high above Strangeland. The wind carried him for miles over its valleys, ravines, and beautiful gardens. The earth beneath him seemed to fade. Kingston's anxiety, stress, and hopelessness were washed away with the wind. He felt a peace that he had not known for a very long time. For the first time, he felt strength. He felt empowered. Kingston knew in his heart that he could continue his life journey.

Soon, the wind settled down to a whispering breeze. Kingston landed softly at the entrance of a garden. He was awakened as a white rose petal brushed across his face before resting on the bridge of his nose. He looked up and before him stood the Herald. "Good morning, Kingston. I have a message for you." He handed Kingston a silver envelope with a red seal. Kingston opened the envelope. Inside was a letter where he found these words:

Dear Kingston:

I heard your cry. I sent the Wind to allow you to experience life above the pain of your affliction. I sent the Wind to bring you comfort. I sent the Wind to let you know that if you place your hope in Me, I will carry you through this season. You see, Kingston, you were riding on Eagles' wings. Let it be a sign of how deeply I care for you. Signed, Adonai

Reflections of the Journey:

1. Have you, like Kingston, felt like your hope in the midst of your affliction was fading? Have you wondered at times, as well, how you will survive? Have you, like Kingston, cried out to God, the only One who truly knows everything about you?

_____

_____

_____

_____

_____

_____

2. In times of despair, what or who did God bring your way to encourage you to continue on your life journey?

_____

_____

_____

_____

_____

_____

Prayer for the Journey:

_____

_____

_____

_____

_____

_____

_____

_____

_____

_____

23

Hope in the All-Knowing God

"They shall run and not be weary; they shall walk and not faith."
Isaiah 40:31

Going through affliction is often similar to being held captive on foreign soil. It is dwelling in the unfamiliar, adapting to what is unnatural, trying to make sense of the unexplainable.

Yet, God, who knows all, is very much aware of where we are. The fact that we are dealing with a *broken-wing* is of no surprise to Him. Nothing is hidden from Him. What is foreign and mystifying to us was known to Him long before it began.

Because of His omniscience, He also knows that because we are from the dust of the earth, we are all subject to weakness and weariness of heart. Regardless of age, the type of affliction, its length, and its depth, the strength and power that we need to rise above it is found in the Everlasting, the Creator, and unfathomable Adonai.

Adonai, the Lord,

"He gives power to the faint, and to him who has no might he increases strength. Even youths shall faint and be weary, and young men shall fall exhausted; but they who wait for the LORD shall renew their strength; they shall mount up with wings like eagles;

they shall run and not be weary; they shall walk and not faint" (Isaiah 40:29-31).

Waiting on the Lord is the key to survival in places like Strangeland. It is to live with eager expectation that He will surely lift us from our lowly place of anxiousness, stress, depression, hopelessness, and fear. Waiting on the Lord will give us new strength and power to look beyond physical limitations. Waiting on the Lord means trusting Him to guide us through deep valleys and on narrow paths. Waiting on the Lord guarantees that, like eagles, we will soar to new heights in Him.

Catching the Wind

When eagles soar, the movement of their pinions is minimal and hardly visible. They use thermals, which are rising currents of warm air and updrafts that enable them to soar above the surface of the earth for hours. They engage in a long-distance migration through a repeated process of mounting high in a thermal and gliding downward to catch the next thermal. The world and its cares are beneath them.

The Wind of God – His Spirit – is invisible but so powerful that He can renew, strengthen, and empower us to face the fierce and sometimes mysterious difficulties of life. Just as the eagle catches thermals to aid its flight when traveling long distances, we too much catch the Wind – get caught up in, grab hold of Him – so that we may attain and maintain our spiritual altitude during the seasons of distress.

We should not cease to pursue the heights of the spiritually abundant life because we are in an unfamiliar place called affliction. An altered life is not a hopeless life. Hopelessness is a state of mind rooted in thoughts that bind us to the effects of our physical circumstances. Hopelessness keeps us from living in the heavenly realm where all of the spiritual blessings in Christ are available. Hopelessness is a thief that robs us of joy and peace.

I spent many days under the weight of hopelessness. Deep within my heart, I knew that God could deliver me at any time. However, when on the next morning's rising I found myself in the same condition, I would be discouraged. I cried rivers of tears, pleading with God to heal me. Then one day, the Wind came blowing and God whispered, *You are not bound by your infirmity, but by your thoughts about your infirmity.*

At first it seemed like a rather odd statement, but it shook me from my feelings and caused me to examine my focal point. The brief examination helped me come to the conclusion that I needed to look up. I needed to rise above the realm of the earth for the strength and the power I needed for the journey. I needed to catch the Wind.

Catching the Wind is getting caught up in His Presence. It requires that we be persistent in our pursuit of Him. Keep praying, keep praising, and keep worshipping. Meditate on the Word of God and let it be your delight.

Physical weakness will come, and so will weariness of heart, but trust Him. Hope in Him and Him alone. When you are weak and weary, catch the Wind – mount up. He will carry you through this season. You are not alone, nor have you been forsaken. You are riding on Eagles' Wings.

Reflections of the Journey:

1. Describe what it means to you to wait upon the Lord.

_____

_____

_____

_____

_____

_____

_____

_____

_____

2. Do you believe that an altered life is not a hopeless life and that hopelessness is a thief that robs its victim of joy and peace? What steps might you take to oppose the thief's attempts to rob you of your joy and peace?

_____

_____

_____

_____

_____

_____

_____

_____

_____

Prayer for the Journey:

_____

_____

_____

_____

_____

_____

_____

_____

_____

_____

24

The Glory in Mortality

"And we all, with unveiled face, beholding the glory of the Lord, are being transformed into the same image from one degree of glory to another. For this comes from the Lord who is the Spirit." 2 Corinthians 3:18

I weighed in at 5 pounds and 10 ounces. I was totally unaware that my growing frame had the capacity to reveal the glory of God. According to man, I wasn't even to be. Years prior, physicians informed my mother that due to a previous tubular pregnancy and its complications, her chances of conceiving a child were impossible. Despite the medical prognosis, I was born approximately five years later between midnight and sunrise on a crisp fall day in November. My timely arrival on earth was a demonstration of God's glory. His sovereignty was revealed; my birth was part of His plan. It was His will.

You were destined to be here. It is God's will. It is His sovereign choice how His glory will be revealed in and through your life. In our mortal state, God's glory is revealed through His ways, character, and grace. His power is demonstrated through our perpetually transformed lives. It is our present hope. In immortality, there is a much greater glory that we will enter into. It is our future hope.

Our Present Hope

Affliction is probably not part of the life you have in mind. It certainly wasn't on my agenda. The same could probably be said by the blind man who Jesus encountered as He went through the holy city of Jerusalem. When the disciples who accompanied Him saw the blind man, they immediately made the assumption that his blindness was a result of his or his parents' sin. Without love and solid facts, and with only a limited understanding of God, their question revealed that they were focused on assigning a reason for this man's physical malady. There were totally unaware that his blindness was the stage for the revelation of God's power.

"Jesus answered, 'It was not that this man sinned, or his parents, but that the works of God might be displayed in him' " (John 9:3).

Jesus made mud out of His saliva and the dust of the earth. He then put it on the man's eyes and sent him to the Pool of Siloam to wash. The young man did as Jesus instructed, and when he returned home he could see. For a man blind from birth to receive his sight was unheard of. It was a demonstration of the miraculous work of God and He was glorified.

When many witness a person's affliction, they may make silent assumptions and judgments attributable to the sin of the person or the sin of generations before. While there can be a connection between sin and suffering, it is not the default answer for all manners of physical affliction.

There are many reasons behind human suffering. Through affliction, God can demonstrate His power so that the eyes of those who are spiritually blind may be opened. God can use suffering to restore hope and confidence in His sovereign ability to work in any and all circumstances. Or, as in Job's case, it could be that God wants us to know that none of us has a perfected understanding of who He is.

Reflections of the Journey:

1. In your affliction, have you ever felt like others have made silent assumptions about your condition or have judged you unfairly? Explain.

_____

_____

_____

_____

_____

_____

_____

_____

2. How has God demonstrated His power through your affliction?

_____

_____

_____

_____

_____

_____

_____

_____

Prayer for the Journey:

_____

_____

_____

_____

_____

_____

_____

_____

_____

_____

25

In the Hands of a Sovereign God

"I had heard of you by the hearing of the ear, but now my eye sees you." Job 42:5

Through the attack of the Sabeans, the fire of God that fell from the heavens, the raid of the Chaldeans, and the breakout of painful boils all over his body, Job found himself in the fire of affliction.

Despite the fact that Job was a servant of God, described as: "A blameless and upright man, who fears God and turns away from evil" (Job 2:3), Job's three friends thought otherwise. Eliphaz, Bildad, and Zophar (members of an ancient society) believed that human suffering was related to and was the penalty for sin.

To the threesome, it was the only logical explanation for Job's suffering. In three rounds of discussion with Job, his three friends tried to convince him that he was being disciplined by God and must accept his punishment. They tried to convince him that no man can be righteous before the almighty God, that his suffering was the direct result of his wickedness, and that he must confess and return to God for restoration.

Job, however, strongly desires the opportunity to speak to God in order to defend his character and prove that his suffering is unjustified. In Chapter 31, Job makes some conclusive remarks to support his innocence. He has not been given to lust nor has he committed adultery. He has maintained his integrity, treated his servants fairly, ministered to the needs of the poor, the widowed, and the fatherless; he has worshipped no false gods; he has not rejoiced in the misfortune of his enemies; he has not refused to provide shelter to someone in need; nor has he withheld wages for the laborers who worked his land (see verses 1-40).

After all of the poetic dialogue, Job's conclusion and speeches from a younger Elihu, God finally responds out of a whirlwind. His first words for Job are found in Job 38:2-3:

"Who is this that darkens counsel by words without knowledge? Dress for action like a man; I will question you, and you make it known to me."

After God questions Job extensively in view of His sovereign power, enormous strength, wisdom, and control over all of creation, Job concedes that he had spoken out of human frailty and fragmented understanding of God. Though Job was an upright man in the eyes of God, what he knew of God was not conclusive. Job's heart was filled with remorse and he repents. Job's spiritual vision, once clouded by his humanity, is now clear. The God that he had only heard of became the God that he could not see (see Job 42:5).

The fire of Job's affliction finally went out. God restored Job and blessed him with fortunes that were double what he had prior to the onset of his devastation. His family and friends came to comfort him and each of them brought him a piece of silver and a gold ring. God blessed Job with 14,000 sheep, 6,000 camels, 1,000 yoke of oxen and 1,000 female donkeys, 7 sons and 3 daughters, and a life span that extended an additional 140 years.

Going through the fire of affliction does not guarantee that the epilogue of our experience will mirror Job's. The final outcome lies within the hands of our sovereign Lord. The fire of affliction can, however, take us to the next level of glory. The key is keeping our hearts and minds focused on God.

Reflections of the Journey:

1. In what ways have you seen God in the midst of your affliction?

_____

_____

_____

_____

_____

_____

_____

_____

2. Are you willing to leave the final outcome of your affliction in the hands of our sovereign God?

_____

_____

_____

_____

_____

_____

_____

Prayer for the Journey:

_____

_____

_____

_____

_____

_____

_____

_____

_____

_____

26

Post-Fire Glory

"I shall come out as gold." Job 23:10

In 1988, the United States Yellowstone National Park, located primarily in the state of Wyoming with portions of it overflowing into the neighboring states of Montana and Idaho, experienced the greatest wildfire in its recorded history. The mosaic fires of Yellowstone raged for several months before they finally came to an end. While much of the visible vegetation was destroyed, the roots underneath the surface were not. Soon afterwards, the ecosystem began the natural process of regeneration.

Some of the plants such as the fireweed, a tall wildflower with distinct pink to purple flowers, began to appear. The lodgepole pine, one of the dominant trees in Yellowstone, produces two types of pine cones, one of which will remain closed and will not open to release and scatter seeds unless it is exposed to fire.

The fire that we go through can begin as a small flicker and expand to proportions of what seems like an out-of-control wildfire. When God allows these flames of affliction to enter our world, no human intervention can circumvent its intensity or length. At the appointed time, however, the raging fire will cease. What remains is the altered state of what was originally there. It is hardly recognizable, if at all, because transformation has taken place.

Like wildfires that are permitted to burn to restore balance to ecosystems, fire has a way of bringing to attention our spiritual imbalances. Once during a time of fellowship with the Lord, He gently whispered to me, *"Often a greater inner healing needs to occur before we see a manifestation of physical healing."* It is in Christ and by the power of His Spirit that this spiritual transformation can take place – burning the stench of our faulty flesh, putting to death our carnal mind and the misdeeds of our mortal bodies.

If God, by His sovereign choice, decides not to heal our physical bodies, there remains a glory that would not have otherwise been revealed had we not passed through the flames of affliction. Because God knows us like no one else, He can see the glory that He desires to be released through us into the earth.

Job understood that God knew him. Job had followed the steps of God, kept His ways, and treasured the word of truth (see Job 23:11-12). Job would not turn away; he would remain faithfully focused on God. Out of all of Job's laments, expressions of bitterness, anguish, and despair, he knew that he would emerge from this fire with spiritual luster, a brilliancy, a greater glory that would have otherwise been dormant had he not been exposed to the flames.

"But He knows the way that I take; when He has tried me, I shall come out as gold." Job 23:10

If you remain in Him, you too shall come out as pure gold. God may be using this fiery experience to release the glory that will serve as the springboard for the next chapter in your life. It may simply be time to turn the page.

Reflections of the Journey:

1. As well as your physical affliction, do you believe there are spiritual areas of your life that need healing? Has the Lord revealed those areas to you?

_____

_____

_____

_____

_____

_____

_____

_____

2. In spite of all that happened to Job in the time of his personal afflictions, he followed the steps of God, kept His ways, and treasured the word of truth. He remained faithfully focused on God, and he came out as pure gold. In what ways are you demonstrating the faithfulness of Job to His faithful God?

_____

_____

_____

_____

_____

_____

_____

Prayer for the Journey:

_____

_____

_____

_____

_____

_____

_____

_____

_____

_____

27

Glory in Immortality – Our Future Hope

"For the things that are seen are temporal, but the things which are not seen are eternal."
2 Corinthians 4:18

Eternity; it is our future hope. It has been spoken, but not yet revealed as it will be. It is assured, but it has not been seen by any man. The patriarchs, by faith, saw it from a distance. Jesus, the Messiah, prophesied about His imminent but unknown time of return. Paul and Peter wrote letters admonishing believers to prepare for His coming. John, through visions and symbolic imagery given on the Isle of Patmos, reveals the splendor of its glory.

Scores of songs have been written about eternity. It has been preached, talked about, and debated. Eternity is " to an inheritance that is imperishable, undefiled, and unfading, kept in heaven for you, who by God's power are being guarded through faith for a salvation ready to be revealed in the last time" (1 Peter 1:4-5). After the fire, the New Jerusalem will descend out of heaven from God. All of creation will cease its groaning. The creation will be liberated from its bondage to decay, and the children of God will receive their imperishable spiritual bodies (see Romans 8:21-23). Both have been subjected to suffering and both will share in the eternal glory.

The temporal agony of suffering and the glorious splendor of the coming eternal kingdom can in no way be compared to one another. They are like two extremes, yet they are inseparable. They are connected by virtue of our sojourn in this life as followers of Christ. Paul writes:

"And if children, then heirs – heirs of God and fellow heirs with Christ, provided we suffer with him in order that we may also be glorified with him. For I consider that the sufferings of this present time are not worth comparing with the glory that is to be revealed to us." (Romans 8:17-18)

Job considered his anguish and miserable suffering as weightier than the sand of the sea (see Job 6:1). A conversation with the Apostle Paul about this matter, however, may have given him a different perspective. Paul would tell him, to the contrary, that his affliction was light and incomparable to the eternal:

"For momentary, light affliction is producing for us an eternal weight of glory far beyond all comparison, while we look not at the things which are seen, but at the things which are not seen; for the things which are seen are temporal, but the things which are not seen are eternal." (2 Corinthians 4:17-18, NASB)

Reflections of the Journey:

1. In the midst of your affliction, are you able to see it from God's eternal perspective? Do you believe that while the affliction you are experiencing may be a heavy burden it cannot be compared with the wonderful glory we will share in eternal life? Explain.

_____

_____

_____

2. Will you consider memorizing or writing out 2 Corinthians 4:17-18 and keeping these verses in your heart and close at hand for your personal encouragement?

_____

_____

_____

_____

_____

Prayer for the Journey:

_____

_____

_____

_____

_____

_____

_____

_____

_____

_____

_____

_____

_____

_____

28

There Awaits a Much Greater Glory

"Having the glory of God, its radiance like a most rare jewel, like a jasper, clear as crystal." Revelation 21:11

In view of Paul's encouraging messages to the church at Rome and the church at Corinth, remember this: The affliction that you are going through is as light as a bird's feather in comparison to the weight of glory that will be revealed in you once Christ returns. Undoubtedly, this is a tough season and at times you may feel like giving up. I want to encourage you; do not give up. Regardless of the grievousness and immensity of your earthly affliction, if you have accepted Christ as your Savior and Lord, your eternal future is secure.

Don't focus on your *broken-wing*. Don't allow it to consume your life. Focus instead on your God, who is able to lift you, sustain you, comfort you, and bless you with the abundance of His peace.

You and I are traveling on a dual path. We are designed and destined to reveal the glory of God during our sojourn in this life and are preparing to forever dwell in the glory that is yet to come.

I am sure you are aware, by virtue of the natural progression of time, that I now weigh more than 5 pounds and 10 ounces. My frame has far exceeded my birth weight. When I stepped from eternity into time on that crisp fall November day, I did not know as I do now that I am here to reveal God's glory. He knew that one day, by His sovereign choice, I would be commissioned to share this story. It is my sincere hope that He be glorified through my *broken-wing.* I remain confident in His promises that there awaits for me a much greater glory.

"And he carried me away in the Spirit to a great, high mountain, and showed me the holy city Jerusalem coming down out of heaven from God, having the glory of God, its radiance like a most rare jewel, like a jasper, clear as crystal. It had a great, high wall, with twelve gates, and at the gates twelve angels, and on the gates the names of the twelve tribes of the sons of Israel were inscribed— on the east three gates, on the north three gates, on the south three gates, and on the west three gates. And the wall of the city had twelve foundations, and on them were the twelve names of the twelve apostles of the Lamb. And the one who spoke with me had a measuring rod of gold to measure the city and its gates and walls. The city lies foursquare, its length the same as its width. And he measured the city with his rod, 12,000 stadia. Its length and width and height are equal. He also measured its wall, 144 cubits by human measurement, which is also an angel's measurement. The wall was built of jasper, while the city was pure gold, like clear glass. The foundations of the wall of the city were adorned with every kind of jewel. The first was jasper, the second sapphire, the third agate, the fourth emerald, the fifth onyx, the sixth carnelian, the seventh chrysolite, the eighth beryl, the ninth topaz, the tenth chrysoprase, the eleventh jacinth, the twelfth amethyst. And the twelve gates were twelve pearls, each of the gates made of a single pearl, and the street of the city was pure gold, like transparent glass. And I saw no temple in the city, for its temple is the Lord God the Almighty and the Lamb. And the city has no need of sun or moon to shine on it, for the glory of God gives it light, and its lamp is the Lamb. By its light will the nations walk, and the kings of the earth will bring their glory into it, and its gates will never be shut by day—and there will be no night there. They will bring into it the glory and the honor of the nations. But nothing unclean will ever enter it, nor anyone who does what is detestable or false, but only those who are written in the Lamb's book of life" Revelation 21:10-27.

Reflections of the Journey:

1. When you're tempted to focus on your *broken-wing*, your affliction, what steps can you take to focus more on the Lord, who is able to lift you, sustain you, comfort you, and bless you with the abundance of His peace?

_____

_____

_____

_____

_____

_____

2. God, your Creator, has a story for you to share, whether spoken or written. What opportunities are available for you to share the wondrous work God is doing in and through you in the midst of the affliction you are experiencing?

_____

_____

_____

_____

_____

Prayer for the Journey:

_____

_____

_____

_____

_____

_____

_____

_____

_____

_____

29

Here I Stand

"As we know, we consider blessed those who have persevered. You have heard of Job's perseverance and have seen what the Lord finally brought about. The Lord is full of compassion and mercy." James 5:11, NIV

Living under the Midwest sky, we experience a myriad of weather conditions. The seasons are often unpredictable. Fall days can be hot and steamy. Summers can range for what is considered normal, mild and rainy to hot and desert-like. A surprising spring-like day can show up in the middle of winter. A snow storm can descend upon us Midwesterners just as daffodils and tulips are peeking above the earth and trees are budding. We have a say in my hometown: "If you don't like the weather, just wait until tomorrow and it will change."

Several years ago, on a spring day – in the season between the vernal equinox and the summer solstice – just as the trees and flowers were beginning to bud, we had an unexpected snowstorm. During the days that followed, my husband and I listened into the night to the sound of cracking tree branches as they separated themselves from our beautiful magnolia tree. The weight of the fallen snow was more than the branches of the budding tree could handle, and before long our front yard was full of tree limbs.

It was weeks before Randall finally got the massive heap of limbs cut up and hauled away. Due to the damage to the tree, we were concerned that it would never bloom again. It did, however, and for many years that followed we have had the pleasure of enjoying the fragrance of its springtime blossoms.

Like the unpredictable weather of the Midwest and the aftermaths that sometime accompany it, our lives are often colored with unpredictable events and their aftermaths. Affliction is one of them.

My journey through affliction has been long, laborious, and filled with many unexpected turns. The weight of this storm has been heavy, but its weight has allowed God to prune from my life – branch by branch – those things which bore no fruit. I am not, however, complete, but I am pressing forward, being conformed to the image of His Son. I am not perfect, but I am pursuing a most perfect God.

My wing has been broken and my life has been altered. In the midst of it all, God has remained constant. Through the aftermath of job loss, a redirected career, financial difficulties, ministry and life changes, I have survived. Because of Him, Here I Stand.

Several years have passed now and the total healing that I desire has not manifested. I have learned, however, not to focus on the passing time but rather on what I do within that time. I choose to focus on God and strive to live the precious gift of life in accordance with His purposes. I choose to allow Him to use my experience with a *broken-wing* to spiritually refine me. I choose to strive to live my life at His pace. I choose to remain in fellowship with the Lord. I choose not to give up! Because of the King of Glory, Here I Stand.

Reflections of the Journey:

1. If your life is altered by your affliction, are you able to identify those things God has pruned from your life as you press forward to become conformed to the image of His Son and to be able to say "Here I Stand" because of Him?

_____

_____

_____

_____

_____

_____

_____

_____

2. What choices are you making to live a life in accordance with God's purposes in spite of your affliction?

_____

_____

_____

_____

_____

_____

_____

_____

Prayer for the Journey:

_____

_____

_____

_____

_____

_____

_____

_____

_____

_____

_____

30

Living in the Present Moment

"Those who trust in the LORD ARE LIKE MOUNT ZION, WHICH CANNOT BE MOVED, BUT ABIDES FOREVER. As the mountains surround Jerusalem, so the LORD SURROUNDS HIS PEOPLE, FROM THIS TIME FORTH AND FOREVERMORE." PSALM 125:1-2

None of us know the details of time that God has not unveiled. He is the only One who knows the end from the beginning. We are only living in the present moment. Regardless of whether your journey through affliction is brief, extended, or declared incurable, God is with you in this present moment.

You have encountered an unexpected cross. As a result, you may feel as if your life is in disarray. Like the unpredictable weather under the Midwest sky, your life may be full of peaks, valleys, and turns. You are not alone; God is with you to bring order to what seems like disorder. His abiding presence is with you in every peak, valley, and at every turn. Your life may have been altered, but it is not over.

Live in the present moment. Embrace the process. Let Him guide you on your journey. Embrace His grace. Live to reflect His glory. Expand your intimacy with Him through prayer and worship. Catch the Wind of His presence.

I am uncertain as to how or when this journey will end, but Here I Stand. Here I Stand, underneath the streams of God's lovingkindness. Here I Stand, embraced by the abundance of His grace. Here I Stand, a testimony of His divine providence. Here I Stand, shielded by His truth. Here I Stand, supported by His enormous strength and power. Here I Stand, in the hands of my Eternal God. What about you? Are you ready to proclaim, "Here I Stand!"

Reflections of the Journey:

1. Can you trust in the knowledge that in your affliction you are not alone, that God is with you to bring order to what seems like disorder? Explain.

_____

_____

_____

_____

_____

2. What will you do to live in the present moment, embrace the process, and let Him guide you on your journey? What can you do to expand your intimacy with the God who loves you and cares about your every need through prayer and worship?

_____

_____

_____

_____

_____

Prayer for the Journey:

_____

_____

_____

_____

_____

_____

_____

_____

_____

_____

About the Author

Phyllls A. Clemons is a teacher of God's word. She has a Bachelor of Science Degree in Administrative Management from the University of Cincinnati and a Master of Religious Education from Cincinnati Bible Seminary. With a call and passion for written communication, Phyllis is the author *of Broken-Wing: Taking the Journey to Spiritual Maturity*, and *Broken-Wing: An Expose' on the Journey Through Affliction*. She and her husband Randall reside in West Chester, Ohio. The have two sons, one grandson, and two granddaughters.

Please visit us at: **www.brokenwingbooks.com**

Follow Phyllls on Twitter and Facebook
@ https://twitter.com/bwings2004 and
https://www.facebook.com/phyllis.clemons.18

Made in the USA
Middletown, DE
04 May 2021

38984807R00075